What People Are Saying about *Yo, Coach!*

"Patrick embodies all the qualities of a great Coach. He was put on this planet to serve his clients and help them achieve their goals. He has the values and culture of what it takes to be a successful business Coach, and his clients benefit as a result. Enjoy the journey as he describes it and take the first step in achieving your goals!"
—Steve Thompson, President and CEO, FocalPoint

"One of the most dangerous things a business owner, entrepreneur, or executive can do today Is to hire a 'coach' without asking many questions about their qualifications. The fact is, 'coach' is a word that almost anyone thinks they can call themselves. But why would you entrust your business and career to someone that you know nothing about? Yo, Coach! tells the reader exactly what a FocalPoint Certified Professional Coach can do for you and the process they use to work with you. You MUST read this book if you're in business or want to be. It describes exactly what you should expect in a great coach. Don't put your business or career at risk. Do it right the first time and hire a FocalPoint Certified Coach."
—Danny Creed, PhD in GSD, Certified Master Business Coach, Certified Executive Coach, named one of the "10 Most Inspiring Transformational Coaches, Globally," Celebrity Coach, and seven-time Brian Tracy Award for Sales Excellence winner

"Patrick has taken away the mystery, unknown, and confusion regarding Business Coaching and what value it delivers to business owners. Patrick communicates effectively the What, How, Why, and Value that business coaching brings to business owners. This book truly exemplifies Google's Chairman Eric Schmidt's statement that "every company needs a Coach."
—Mark R. Steinke, Elite Master Business Coach and Coach to three of the Top 100 Fastest-Growing Companies in Philadelphia, 2023

YO, COACH!

How Professional Coaching Transforms Your Business Dreams into a Winning Gameplan

Patrick Clancey

Printed in the United States of America
Published in Hellertown, PA

ISBN 978-1-958711-91-0
Library of Congress Control Number 20239222972

For more information or to place bulk orders, contact the author or the publisher at Jennifer@BrightCommunications.net.

To my beautiful wife and life-partner, Amy,
who brought me back home, brought me back to
God and brought me to coaching.

"I don't know where I'd be if I didn't have you...
Thank God I Do."
—Lauren Daigel

Contents

Foreword

The most important part of business success is the ability to consistently generate sales and profitability. You have probably heard of the Pareto Principle, or the "80/20 Rule." This rule says that 80 percent of the companies in any business struggle to split a meager 20 percent of the profits that are paid in that business. Meanwhile, the top 20 percent of businesses earn 80 percent of the profits, often 5 to 10 times as much as the other companies, even though they are selling very much the same product or service to the same customers in the same market. Why is this?

Very often, the reason businesses are functioning below their financial potential is simply that they do not know what they do not know. As a result, they are unable to correct what they are doing, or not doing, because they don't know which levers to pull. My life's work as a speaker, trainer, and consultant to more than 1,000 large companies and more than 10,000 small and medium-sized companies in 22 different countries over the past 40 years has proven that often, it takes only very small changes in the day-to-day activities of a company to achieve huge changes in profitability. This can happen to you as well. If you know what to change.

Patrick Clancey, a top FocalPoint coach, has been thoroughly trained in the FocalPoint Way and has worked with hundreds of entrepreneurs and small business owners. He knows the critical factors, those "small things" you have to do first if you want to be successful. Over the time that you work with Patrick, which can be from several months to several years depending on the needs of your business, he can save your business many months or even years in achieving the level of profitability and personal income that drove you to start your small business in the first place!

Peter Drucker, the management guru, once said that the single most important factor in business is results. With FocalPoint coaching, we concentrate single-mindedly on helping you become absolutely clear about the results that you want and need to attain for your business. In Yo, Coach! Patrick Clancey outlines a practical, proven process to help you clearly identify where you are now, where you want to go, the very best way of getting there, and how to achieve the results that are most important to your success in the months and years ahead.

This amazing book opens your eyes and your mind to an entire series of activities engaged in by the most successful businesses. Patrick, as a professional and experienced business coach, explains how coaching will help you to implement these ideas in every part of your business—and achieve dramatic results faster than you ever thought possible.

Congratulations! You are about to embark on one of the great experiences of business: achieving your financial goals and everything that this means to you, your employees, and your family. And, like all of our great FocalPoint coaches, Patrick will be with you every step of the way.

—Brian Tracy, world-renowned speaker, mentor, growth specialist, author of more than 70 books in 28 languages, and co-founder of FocalPoint

Introduction

As a friend, father, businessperson, Coach, and leader, I've always believed, and found, that staying true to my values, our values, has been the key to successful outcomes—my "true north." True north is defined, it doesn't change, it points directly to the geographic north pole no matter where you are or what the circumstance. In life, the reference to my true north has the same galvanizing power: It doesn't change, it's always true. Making decisions, whether advising my children, working with a Coach, leading a company, or even playing a sport, should always be in alignment with my true north.

At FocalPoint, we have a team of incredible Coaches, hundreds of them, and they're driven by purpose and serving their clients—that's their true north. We hop out of bed with a skip in our step knowing we'll be working with amazing people, in fantastic companies, all over the world. We're here to serve our clients and help them achieve their goals, and in doing so, we achieve ours.

As president and CEO of FocalPoint, my most important duty is to ensure we onboard the right people, the Coaches who fit this purpose and drive toward true north. In meeting Coach Patrick Clancey, we knew we had the right team member from the start. Patrick embodies all the qualities of a great Coach and was put on this planet to serve his clients and help them achieve their goals. He has the values and culture of what it takes to be a successful business Coach, and his clients benefit as a result.

It's an honor to be on the same team with Patrick. Enjoy the journey as he describes it and take the first step in achieving your goals!

Gratefully,
Steve Thompson

Chapter 1

I Know What a Doctor Does, But...a Business Coach? (What's a Business Coach?)

"No one lives long enough to learn everything they need to learn starting from scratch. To be successful, we absolutely, positively have to find people who have already paid the price to learn the things that we need to learn to achieve our goals."–Brian Tracy

I've always loved public speaking, and I happily grab the mic any chance I get. When coaching is the topic of the day, I often ask the audience, "Who here knows what a doctor does?" Hands will quickly shoot up, and people will confidently declare things like, "They treat sick people!" or, "They diagnose what is wrong with you!" or, "They figure out what's ailing you and prescribe what you need to get better!"

Then I'll ask, "Who here knows what a business coach does?" An awkward hush will typically fall over the room as the audience members look at each other and squirm uncomfortably in their seats. To be fair, most folks can't be expected to know what a business coach does because few people have actually worked with one. Along the same lines, I couldn't tell you what an astrophysicist does because astrophysics isn't really part of my life.

Yet, in many ways a business coach and a doctor aren't too dissimilar. Typically, my clients know that "something's not quite right," but they are not quite sure what exactly is wrong. They often know where it hurts, but they aren't quite sure why it hurts. Discomfort has grown into outright pain, and they can no longer hope that it's just going to go away. That's usually when they reach out and yell, "Yo, Coach!"

It's been said that business coaching is the art of asking good questions. Like a trained physician, a certified business coach will start with some basics like taking your temperature and recording your blood pressure. Then he'll ask things like where does it hurt and how long has it been hurting? Finally, he'll poke and prod here and there and order some tests. The difference is, in the case of the business coach, the "patient" is your small business.

Some businesses are only slightly sputtering, and a short course of medication will help them breathe easier. In other cases, the obvious pain is merely the symptom of the true malady, and health can only be restored via more thorough investigation and a multi-pronged treatment plan. Regardless, just as modern medicine is geared toward "preventative medicine," business coaching focuses on "organizational wellness." An expert business coach anticipates the next challenges that might beset the business and helps his client build the core strength and robust business immune system needed to remain healthy, come what may.

So, what does a business coach do? He asks questions, listens, and guides his client along a path that promotes good corporate health, peak performance, and a positive environment for all of the company's stakeholders, be they the owners, the employees, the employee's families, the company's customers or its suppliers.

Patrick Clancey

Improvement In Action

Start — What Aren't You Doing Now That You Would Be Better 'Doing'?

Stop — What Are You Doing Now That You Would Be Better 'Not Doing'?

Continue — What Are You Doing Now That You Should 'Keep Doing'?

The FocalPoint Start…Stop…Continue framework is a perfect example of the type of excellent questions your coach will use to help you distill meaningful insight from the clutter and chatter that submerges many small businesses. Start…Stop…Continue is one proven technique that your Certified FocalPoint Business Coach will use to ensure you remain focused on those activities that deliver the most to your business.

Chapter 2

Heavy Is the Head that Wears the Crown (Am I the Only One Struggling to Run My Small Business?)

"I've found that luck is quite predictable. If you want more luck, take more chances. Be more active. Show up more often."—Brian Tracy

In his 1981 classic *History of the World, Part I*, Mel Brooks gave us the iconic catchphrase "It's good to be king!" Nowhere is this more true than in the world of small business. Small business owners set their own hours, call their own shots, and don't report to anyone. Plus, they are the chief beneficiary of all their efforts! Come up with a great idea, work hard, do more things right than wrong, and the world is your oyster. Just look at Jeff Bezos. Or Jay-Z. Or the HVAC guy living in the big house down the road driving his beautiful wife around in his sports car! I want a great business and a great life, too! Sign me up!

That's the fantasy. The reality is that running a small business isn't easy. I know. I've owned three of them. I've felt the cold sweats that come over you when you know you can't make payroll on Friday. I know what it's like to be staring at the ceiling at 3 a.m., knowing that tomorrow you have to lay off a staff member who has worked for you for ten years, someone who can be trusted, and someone who you will see at soccer practice tomorrow afternoon because his kid plays on the same team as yours. I know the dread of realizing you have to tell your spouse you need to sell an asset to pump the money into the business. And the dread of having to pluck up the courage to assure her that you'll make the money back, even though you know your circumstances are full of risks and the money might never come back. Yes, the small business owner gets all the rewards, but he also assumes all the risks.

Small business owners are part banker, part decision-maker, and part cheerleader. You fund operations. You make not only the hard decisions, but *all* the decisions. And you do your best to keep morale high around the office. Still sound easy? Shakespeare's King Henry IV knew that "uneasy is the head that wears a crown." Henry's lament applies equally to the small business owner because all of that alluring glory of being your own boss comes with a pricetag that regular employees never see.

Small business owners certainly carry more stress than their salaried counterparts. They also live in greater isolation. Small business owners are full-time poker players. No one, and I mean no one—not staff, not vendors, and certainly not customers—can ever see your company's true circumstances reflected on your face. For the business owner, coworkers can be buddies, but they can't be confidantes. Many small business owners are even reluctant to share their cares with their spouses. They tell themselves things like, "I don't want to bring my work home," or, "I don't want to be *that guy* who only talks about business," but the reality is that they know their problems are real, and they don't want to transfer their stress onto a loved one.

Enter your business coach. Your business coach listens and assesses, but never judges. Your business coach knows the emotions that course through the business owner's body each and every day. Your coach is a safe zone for sharing your burdens. The first benefit of every coaching relationship is the "I get you" understanding that the coach brings. Everything shared with your coach is received and kept in complete confidence. Your coach is the only person you don't have to play poker with. Your coaching sessions form that sacred space where you can, and MUST, be completely open and candid. The very success of your business absolutely demands it!

Your business coach is your beacon of direction. Certified FocalPoint business coaches are experts at helping you simplify your goals and plans. They will help you distinguish between tactics and strategy. Also, they will assist you in harnessing strategic analytical tools such as SWOT analysis, Riccardo's Law, and the Pareto Principle to design robust strategies that ensure your business's success.

Business owners know that the decisions they make impact their businesses and also the lives of their employees (and *their* families) as well. Imagine the relief you will feel when you know with confidence that the decisions you are making will lead your business toward lasting success. Imagine knowing (100 percent!) that you are doing the right thing for yourself and your team. With a skilled business coach, you're never alone in decision-making. Working with your business coach will silence your inner critic and give you the confidence that you are navigating your company's challenges like the leader you know you are. Coaching brings you certainty!

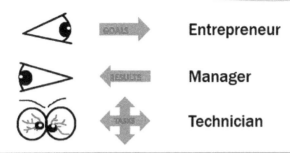

In his famous book *The E-Myth Revisited*, Michael Gerber outlined the idea that all small business owners need to view their operations through three different sets of eyes: the eyes of the Entrepreneur, the Manager, and the Technician. Small business owners don't have the luxury of playing just one role in their organizations, and they must flip between these three different roles, usually many times in the same day. Your Certified FocalPoint Business Coach will help you understand each of these roles and guide you to ensuring that you and each of your team members spend your time where your unique skills add the greatest value to your organization.

Chapter 3

Your Coach Is Your Nonequity Partner
(What Are the Benefits of Business Coaching?)

"The key to success is action."—Brian Tracy

You are active. Creative. A go-getter. Always have been. You have ideas and a strong sense of doing things right. You are good at what you do. You know it inside and out. That's how you came to be running your own business, or maybe why you became an entrepreneur blazing a new trail.

Your business was born out of foresight, drive, and the bright spark of a good idea. It continues to exist because you are uniquely qualified to combine those things in a way no one else can. Maybe you were the first to see some mind-blowing technological breakthrough. Or maybe it's how you listen, how you smile, or how you train your people to deliver world-beating customer service. Your business exists because you are really good at delivering something your customers can't get anywhere else. But can you make a profit at it? To use a simple analogy, being able to produce amazing brownies is a necessary part of having a successful bake shop, but that alone is not enough. You need to be able to make a profit doing it!

Virtually all entrepreneurs and most small business owners start their businesses because they excel at "doing the do." A seamstress is highly competent at sewing and a computer programmer is excellent at writing elegant code. Unfortunately, it's pretty uncommon to be exceptionally skilled in your area of expertise *and* be a world-beating business maven. In fact, the green-eyed monster that eats up most sterling business ideas is an insufficient understanding of how that good idea translates to profit—how it magically transforms the number of dollars you put in into a far greater number of dollars you get out. The entrepreneur's spark is a vital component in this process, but injecting business acumen is essential to the alchemy.

Where do you find that piece of the puzzle? You can bring in a partner who spent his days studying business instead of dreaming up good ideas, but that means you will no longer own 100 percent of the company. It also means that some portion of the control over the direction of the company will no longer rest with you. That path might one day lead to an unresolvable conflict that could potentially doom your small business. Alternatively, you can do what larger companies do and hire a phalanx of professionals who can deliver on their areas of expertise. For example, you can hire someone who is good at sales and marketing, an HR exec who can help with personnel, even add a finance wiz to handle all the money stuff. But can you afford really great people in each of those areas? Or will reality force you to take the risk of hiring the level of skills you can afford rather than the level of skills your business needs to succeed?

The solution? It might be a pretty good time to yell, "Yo, Coach!"

Your Certified FocalPoint Business Coach brings outstanding expertise in clarity, direction, hiring, sales, time management, prioritization, and strategy. All in one person. Your coach will help you navigate your finances, sales, hiring, and your strategic positioning—all while allowing you to make 100 percent of the final decisions and retain 100 percent of your company's ownership—and profit! That's what we mean when we say 'your coach is your non-equity partner.'

FocalPoint coaches are a select breed. Each Certified FocalPoint business coach has accumulated a wealth of talent and experience during an impressive career in business prior to becoming a coach. Then, FocalPoint layers in the proven business acumen of Brian Tracy, the most-listened-to author on business success in the world, and a plain-speaking coaching curriculum developed by Campbell Fraser, to arm every coach with an impressive arsenal of weapons for defeating a cradle-to-grave array of business problems. Plus, FocalPoint coaches are a collaborative group, who freely exchange their insights and solutions with their coaching peers. Your coach can, and will, liberally tap into this network to bring the best, freshest insights to his work with you. When you sign one FocalPoint Coach, in many ways you get them all!

Working tirelessly from dawn till dusk? Feeling overwhelmed, stressed, and frustrated because your efforts don't seem to translate into the growth and success you envisioned? Tired of being the only person your customers want to work with, feeling like you're doing everything yourself? Facing challenges assembling a team that truly aligns with your vision and values? Frustrated by your sales team's inability to meet targets and deliver on their promises? Wondering why even experienced sales professionals struggle to achieve results in your company? Struggling with motivation and paralyzed by stress?

It's time to shout "Yo, Coach!" and team up with a nonequity partner who can help you overcome these issues, deliver extraordinary value on your investment, and walk with you every step of the way so that you can spend more time doing what you do best!

The Way to Wealth

Leads
X Conversion Rate
= CUSTOMERS

X Avg $ per Sale
X No. Sales / Period
= REVENUE

- Cost of Goods Sold
- Operating Costs
= PROFIT

Brian Tracy's Way-to-Wealth formula highlights the six elements that lead to profit generation for any business entity. Your Certified FocalPoint Business Coach will help you identify the levers in your business that make up these elements and provide you with laser guidance on how to optimize your business profit by optimizing each individual element.

Chapter 4

Grandma Knew You Get What You Pay For! (Why Do I a Need a *Certified* Business Coach?)

"Your greatest asset is your earning ability. Your greatest resource is your time."—Brian Tracy

"Lemme give you some free advice, and remember, it's worth every penny you pay for it!" That sounds like a line from a comedy routine, but like many things your grandma knew instinctively, it is in fact 100 percent true.

Who do you talk to when you are unclear about the direction of your business? You might have an uncle who made a fat stack in his day. You might let your concerns spill out to the total stranger on the next bar stool or next airplane seat whose one or two comments suddenly make him or her seem like the most intelligent person on the planet. I've been guilty of talking out loud about my business woes to my faithful canine companion. These are but some of the sources of free advice available to a small business owner struggling with the isolation that is part of the job description. While some sources of advice are ridiculous, others are at least a little sagacious.

Jokes aside, I've been blessed to have been taken under the wing of competent mentors at many different stages of my life. Their guidance and heartfelt concern taught me lessons that remain with me to this day. The problem is that the wisdom of your successful uncle or even my competent mentors was confined to a specific area of acumen and based on the prevailing conditions of those times. They taught me the value of wise counsel, but none of them had the full breadth of knowledge *my* business needed in *my* era. And none of them ever had the one thing I truly needed: a holistic plan.

A Certified FocalPoint business coach provides guidance based on modules that carry your business from foundation to exit. First, we start with clarity: your *why*. We help you build and internalize deep clarity around what you do, why you do it, and who you do it for. It is not at all uncommon for business owners who *think* they know their why to discover that their vision isn't quiet as laser-focused as they thought or that no one in the organization actually aligns with it.

Next, your coach will help you build a rock-solid cultural *foundation* that is actually lived by your team. This foundation will deliver value by acting as the touchpoint for many of the important decisions in your company's future.

After that, your coach will take a deep, hard look at effectiveness: your *how*. You'll systematically raise your organization's efficiency by examining your execution to ensure that you do what you do, better. Your coach will question, test, and assess until you have absolute certainty that every aspect of your operation is performing at its peak. You will *know* that everything you are doing is right.

Once you and your coach know what's right, you'll focus on how to do *more* of what you do. That's *growth*. Your coach will help you grow, in part, by helping you understand why your customers patronize your business and how your products satisfy their needs. Your revenues will grow because your customers will have conviction around your products and services. Regardless of whether yours is an organization that likes to use this word or not, that's "sales."

Finally, with your coach, you will develop a *strategy:* a well-demarcated path that extends far into the future and even fully considers your exit from the business. Why? Because the only thing that is inevitable once you enter a business, is that one day you will exit your business. When that will happen and how that will happen is up to you. You might choose to take on a partner to share the load and the risk. You might pass the business on to the next generation. You might eventually sell the business outright by taking the business public or combining with another industry player. You might even decide that the business has fully served all your needs and simply shut it down. But one way or another, just as you entered, you will one day exit.

Your coach will begin talking to you about your exit *very* early. Why? First, your business will only be optimized to attract top value if all your decisions have been aligned with that objective from the beginning. And second, because life happens. A life-changing event can occur for any of us at any time. Such an event might completely alter your ability to continue to run your small business. Should that day ever come, you will need your business to already be positioned to deliver the best value possible and not be traded at a fire sale price. By optimizing for exit from the beginning, you will sleep well, knowing that you have done the best for yourself and for your loved ones should anything unfortunate happen.

Want to know what "exit" means to me? I tell my clients that the definition of "exit" is to have the ability to step out of your successful business to pursue whatever dream you identify, *without* in any way damaging your successful business. That's the "exit" every small business owner should be navigating toward.

Systematic, professional coaching that can deliver these results isn't free, but it isn't an expense, either. It's an investment that offers high returns. If your business needed a machine or other productive asset to help you get to the next level, you wouldn't hesitate to buy it. You would gladly type in your credit card numbers, knowing that your investment and much more (the return on the investment) would soon be landing in your bank account. Coaching is no different. A study commissioned by the international Coach Federation (ICF) and conducted by PriceWaterhouse Coopers and Association Resource Centre Inc. (ICF Global Coaching Client Study, 2009) revealed that companies who invested in coaching gained a median return of seven times their initial investment. The direct and indirect benefits of coaching are shown in the graphic on the opposite page.

FocalPoint has documented countless case studies of clients who have achieved amazing financial results by implementing strategies developed together with their coaches. Your coach will be more than happy to share one or more case studies with you that has parallels to your current challenges or industry.

Our proven track record of success explains why even healthy, thriving companies invest in business coaching. For example, Tiger Woods is arguably the most successful competitor in the history of professional golf, yet he has retained a swing coach throughout his professional career. Google as a business entity has rocketed from a college dorm idea to one of the world's most profitable companies that has literally touched the lives of everyone on the planet. Yet, Eric Schmidt, the Chairman of Google, has experienced so much benefit from his business coach that he has repeatedly said that *every* company should have a business coach!

Similarly, not all companies that explore coaching are experiencing difficulty. Many simply want to go further, faster. And more easily. They want to move from good to great and leverage their strengths in ways that create chasms of difference between them and their nearest competitors. These formidable entities use their coaches to grow from strength to strength. They prize their coaches and take pride in working with only the very best.

Your coach is not in the "promise" business, so he is never going to market any specific "return" to you. Success is never guaranteed because the outcome of coaching depends to a very large extent on the level of effort expended by the client. Still, the performance data speaks for itself. Your coach delivers value. The rest is up to you.

What's the value of coaching? It's knowing. Knowing you have a plan. Knowing your team is delivering. Knowing that every action you take today is building the tomorrow you have set your sights on. No stress. No uncertainty. Knowing.

When you work together with a FocalPoint business coach, you get what you pay for—and a whole lot more!

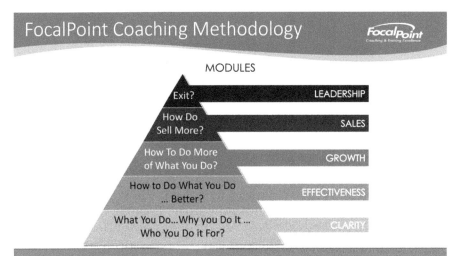

FocalPoint Business Coaching is based upon a modular curriculum that is designed to ensure our clients develop a deep understanding of every aspect of their business from foundation to exit. FocalPoint offers a similar approach to its Executive Coaching, Group Coaching, and Leadership Programs.

Chapter 5

The Player Shoots the Foul Shot
(What's the Coaching Process Like?)

You have to put in many, many, many tiny efforts that nobody sees or appreciates before you achieve anything worthwhile."—Brian Tracy

Basketball coaches love it when their players get fouled because their team is almost guaranteed free points. Toward the end of many basketball games, the team that's behind in the game will have no choice but to foul the opposing team player to conserve the dwindling game clock. The best coaches will intentionally get the ball into the hands of their best foul shooters so that their high-percentage players take those free throws. The pressure might be on and the arena may be alive with deafening crowd noise, but the coach is calm on the sidelines because he knows his players are well trained and can execute under pressure. The player still has to take the foul shot, but the coach is virtually certain the ball will go in the basket.

How do we make sure this happens in your business? It's all about conversations. I highlighted in Chapter 1 that a coach's job is to ask excellent questions, and that's where we begin. A sound coaching relationship has to pass through three distinct phases before both parties are convinced that the coaching relationship will be successful.

The first phase involves one or more short conversations we call Discovery. This is how the coach becomes familiar with the basics of your business at a high level: what you do, why you are good at it, and where you stand relative to your competition.

In the second phase, the coach will dig deeper in a 20-Minute Coaching Session. He'll get a clear picture of exactly where your business is today, where you would like it to be in the future, and exactly when you would like it to be there. You will need to get used to that word "exactly" because coaches are all about precision, not generalities. It's necessary to drive our clients to certainty, not "sorta." This conversation will involve establishing concrete goals and timelines. The goals will be your goals, not the coach's. It's where *you* want to be and when *you* want to be there.

This second phase of your explorations will also involve a frank discussion around the specific obstacles that stand between your business and the goals you have identified. To overcome an obstacle, it must first be identified, and the coach will ask questions around lots of different areas where obstacles might be hindering your progress. Then the coach will explore the impact of reaching your goal. What will reaching your goal mean for your business? How will it change the way your company operates in the marketplace? What will attaining your stated goal mean for you personally? What new gateways will it open for your life? What dreams will it help you realize? Might it create new challenges? How can we address those factors as well when considering our way forward? That's an excellent question! As I mentioned, it's the coach's job to ask a lot of excellent questions.

We call the third phase of the process the Strategic Business Review (SBR). It involves a critical evaluation of the biggest roadblocks you will likely face along the path to your stated goals and how they might best be overcome. In the SBR, the coach will reveal an outline of the path that he knows will allow your company to reach your goals. The coach might share a universally applicable business concept—in FocalPoint we call them "Power Principles"—that broadly describes the current state of your business. He may also want to show you "The Way to Wealth" by doing some "worked examples" around your company's sales or profits. The SBR can take an hour or longer, and sometimes it needs to be spread across two different meetings. However, the SBR is essential because it will allow you to begin to see the value the coach will deliver for your business.

Notice that throughout this three-phase process, I have used the term *the* coach, not *your* coach. While both parties are moving through this process, neither of you have decided that a relationship makes sense yet. While you are focused on determining whether the coach can help address your concerns, the coach is busy assessing you. There is a limit to the number of clients the coach can work with at any given time. Therefore, the coach needs to convince himself that you are committed to the change you wish to achieve and are fully prepared to expend the effort needed to enact the process improvements identified. He needs to decide that he wants to invest his efforts in you.

It is only after the SBR, when you have a clear picture of the value the coach will bring to you and the coach has developed confidence that you are committed to change and growth, that a decision will be made to commence a coaching relationship. This only happens when both parties are convinced that the relationship will create value. The decision will be mutual. The whole process has been designed to lead to this conclusion. Either the relationship makes sense, or it doesn't. And when you both agree that it does, *the* coach becomes *your* coach. Not your best friend. Your coach. Your business accountability partner.

The first step in your coaching journey will likely involve an assessment of your individual behavioral characteristics, motivational driving forces, and communication style. Such an assessment will help your coach understand you as a person and optimize his coaching delivery to suit your most comfortable style and the way you learn most efficiently. It will also undoubtedly provide you with valuable insights into how you interact with the people in your world.

Next up will be an informal induction session where your coach will explain how the coaching process will unfold in terms of scheduling, delivery, expectations of weekly inputs and progress, application exercises, and tracking. For a successful coaching relationship to unfold, it is critical that the coach and the business owner be in sync on the requirements and expectations of the coaching process. Coaching is a two-way process. Your coach will invest a great deal of time, effort, and mental energy into helping you succeed, and he will expect the same from you. As mentioned above, the business owner–not the coach–shoots the foul shot and must be totally committed to the coaching process if he wants to rack up the points on the scoreboard.

With the basics now firmly in place, you and your coach will take a deep dive into your goals and what their achievement will mean to the financial health of your company and to you personally. Coaching is all about specifics, so be prepared to keep drilling down until detailed, realistic outcomes are identified and the motivations behind them are clear. Vague generalities such as "It would be great if we could increase sales" won't be accepted as your goal. Your coach is sure to ask, "By how much?" And if you reply, "How about double?" you can expect your coach to ask, "Where exactly does *double* come from? Might a 25 percent increase be more realistic? Or should the target really be *triple*, instead of double?"

Such questions will help you hone the "what" of your goal until it's realistic, if slightly uncomfortable. Next, you will collaboratively break that goal down into the specific steps that need to be taken to get there. These steps will be quantified and translated into performance metrics that can be measured and assessed. In your coaching relationship, you will revisit these metrics regularly because you will never know where you are in your journey unless you understand how far you've come and how much further you need to travel to reach your destination. This is the "how" of your journey. But you won't be done with your goal-setting until you and your coach also agree on the why. What will be the tangible benefits of attaining your goal? What will it create for you? What will it enable you to do that you can't do today? And what future goal comes within reach when attaining this goal builds a new, higher platform for you to stand on?

This exercise is about *your* goals. It's not about what the coach thinks might be good for your company. It's about the firm, concrete targets you want to hit in an identified period of time. Sure, your coach will provide guidance and will ask the questions that will help you crystalize your thoughts, but the targets and timelines are always set by the business owner. You decide the destination and when you need to be there. The coach will then apply his knowledge and experience to craft a plan that will help you get there. That plan will then become the roadmap for your future coaching journey.

In sports, a good coach enters each contest with a unique game plan that his experience tells him will likely yield success. But he knows he needs to stay flexible and willing to make some strategic changes to suit new conditions as the game unfolds. The same is true in business coaching. The dynamics of any small business can change every day. The economy changes. Staff come and go. New regulations come into force. And your company most definitely will change as a result of the actions you take from what you discover in your coaching. This means your coaching gameplan may need to be modified, and your coach is capable of doing that. Reviews and assessments are part of coaching, and you will engage in them regularly. You and your coach will agree on course adjustments that keep you on track to reach your goal.

But coaching is flexible in another way, too! The business environment is dynamic, and sometimes the unexpected happens. Crises are crises, and they need to be met skillfully and immediately to keep the overall mission on track. Imagine that you and your coach are making great strides in the area of business simplification and delegation, when suddenly, your sales manager resigns. As you enter your next coaching session, you might say, "Coach, I know we're supposed to be applying Occam's Razor today, but last night my sales manager came into my office and said she needs to quit her job to care for an elderly parent who can no longer look after herself. I'm excited about streamlining our operations, but I can't think of anything else until I find a new sales manager!" Your coach will immediately switch gears and begin to guide you on behavioral styles, roles/responsibilities, and all the other considerations that will help you find a new sales manager who is completely aligned with your company's values and direction and who can perform to the level your goals require.

Armed with a clear understanding of your what, your how, and your why–and with a course of action set that you can be sure will take you to your destination–you'll be ready to peel off your sweats and start to do your stretches. You're about to become an expert foul shooter!

The Sigmoid Curve

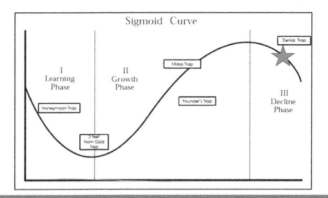

The Harvard Business School and others have elucidated that all businesses proceed through a predictable lifetime consisting of three distinct phases, namely, the Learning Phase, the Growth Phase, and the Decline Phase. Typically, the performance of any business can be represented using an S-shaped, or Sigmoid, Curve. Common challenges that businesses face as they move along their maturation process include the Honeymoon Trap, the 3-Feet From Gold Trap, the Founder's Trap, the Midas Trap, and the Denial Trap. Your Certified FocalPoint Business Coach will help you identify where exactly your business is today, how to address your current challenge, and how to prepare to avoid or successfully deal with the next trap your business can anticipate facing.

Chapter 6

Brian Tracy? He Sounds Familiar!
(Why Should I Use the FocalPoint Way?)

"Successful people are simply those with successful habits."
—Brian Tracy

As an author of more than eighty books and one of the world's most accomplished public speakers, Brian Tracy is an inspirational management guru and thought leader extraordinaire! After a business career that included work with such notable organizations as IBM, Arthur Andersen, McDonnell Douglas, and the Million Dollar Round Table, Brian moved on to become the leading coach on leadership, management, sales, personal development, strategic planning, goal-setting, self-esteem, and time management. He is a dynamic, entertaining speaker who reaches more than half a million people each year. Brian informs and inspires his audiences to peak performance and high levels of achievement. He has produced more than 400 different audio and video learning programs, covering the entire spectrum of human and corporate performance.[1]

Brian Tracy and partner Campbell Fraser adapted the very best of Brian's entrepreneurial and professional development learnings and strategy into the FocalPoint coaching and training process. This allows business owners, leaders, and their teams to effectively leverage Brian's business building tools, systems, and methodology for maximum benefit.

Literally thousands of companies have successfully employed the FocalPoint Way. FocalPoint coaches utilize these proven methods and systems, custom tailored to their clients' circumstances, to reveal new ways of approaching business issues and finding new opportunities. We help you craft strategies that might been previously obscured by the day-to-day grind.

The FocalPoint Way is to apply a laser focus on four critical parts of your business: vision, strategy, understanding and success.

Vision: The FocalPoint Way starts with a focus on your vision. What is your vision for your business, for you personally, and for your family? Where do you want to be one year from now? How about five or ten years? Your FocalPoint coach will help you identify your vision and engrain it at the heart of your business.

Strategy: Next, your FocalPoint coach will help you identify the most important factors and the optimal business strategies needed to achieve your goals. We work with you one-on-one, helping you concentrate your efforts in the most meaningful, productive areas of your company.

Understanding: An important part of the FocalPoint coaching process is education, helping you gain a crystal-clear understanding of where you are today, what resources you have available, and what obstacles you anticipate encountering on the path to reaching your goals. We focus on quantifiable results, tracking and measuring key metrics so you can clearly see the gains you are making toward your goals and know that you are doing what's right for your business.

Success: With a clear vision, strategy, and an understanding of what you will need to achieve your goals, you can begin driving forward to create that vision. Your FocalPoint coach is your confidant, mentor, and guide along that journey, helping you leverage your strengths, improve upon areas for development, and realize previously unimagined gains across multiple areas of your company.

Regardless of whether the challenge you are facing relates to time, teams, money, or exit strategy, a Certified FocalPoint business coach will provide the experience, outside perspective, and proven systems needed to provide quantifiable performance results!

---

[1] With special thanks to Entrepreneur Medial LLC, The Heritage Foundation, and FocalPoint International Inc. for biographical information on Brian Tracy and detailed information on FocalPoint.

INTERNATIONAL BESTSELLER
MORE THAN 1.5 MILLION COPIES SOLD

EAT THAT FROG!

21 GREAT WAYS TO STOP PROCRASTINATING AND GET MORE DONE IN LESS TIME

THIRD EDITION
Updated with Two New Chapters

BRIAN TRACY

In his seminal work *Eat that Frog*, Brian Tracy outlined how to avoid procrastination and achieve outcomes greater than you ever thought imaginable. Brian's secret lies in simply identifying your "frog"— the task you face that has the greatest consequences on your business or life–and ensuring you "eat it" (or do it) first thing every day. Your Certified FocalPoint Business Coach knows that making a habit of accomplishing your most impactful task, the one you are most likely to put off, every single day will provide you with both immediate satisfaction and long-term success.

Chapter 7

Who the Heck Is Patrick Clancey?
(Okay, I'm Ready for a Coach, But Why You?')

"Successful people are always looking for opportunities to help others. Unsuccessful people are always asking, 'What's in it for me?'"—Brian Tracy

I vividly recall waking up at the Peninsula Hotel in Manila one morning in the early 1990s and seeing a white letter-sized envelope on the carpet just inside my hotel room door. Envelopes like that were common in those pre-internet pre-cellphone days and signaled that a facsimile, or fax, had arrived at the hotel business center while you were sleeping. As an expatriate working in Asia for an American company, I received overnight faxes almost daily because the standard business day for our California headquarters largely took place while I was sleeping. The ritual of reading the morning fax traffic was as ingrained in me as looking at the headlines in the daily paper. It represented the passing of the baton, as the business day moved from America to Asia. That evening, I would be on the other side of the ritual, closing out my day by sending similar communiques to colleagues in Europe whose day would be starting around the time mine would be ending. Such was the cadence of information flow back then.

But that morning's envelope contained a heart-stopping shock. Its terse message said the company had been declared insolvent while I was asleep. There would be no payroll that week, and the company credit cards that I used to settle all my travel expenses had been frozen. I was out of a job, a long way from home and financially stranded.

Jobs were extremely scarce in my field in the United States at that time and, as a foreigner, I was unemployable overseas. The only realistic option I had was to start my own company and owing to certain legal requirements find a way to employ myself.

Becoming an entrepreneur wasn't my plan. It was my necessity.

Over the ensuing years, I went on to start three companies, all in the infrastructure space. One was a dismal failure that I allowed to bleed money for far too long. That brainchild taught me the invaluable lesson that your business must always be run by your head, never your heart. The second business served its unique purpose and was shuttered without much in the way of either profit or loss. The remaining company is still operating today, albeit without much involvement from me.

So, when it comes to small business and entrepreneurial spirit, my understanding isn't theoretical. It's hard-earned. I know the journey my clients are on because I've walked it. I've breathed it. And I've paid the tuition fee. I was blessed to have had a few mentors along the way, who helped me steer clear of a few craters. But mostly, my advances came from trial and error and at a cost paid in stress and compromised personal relationships.

I loved my journey, and I wouldn't trade it for anything. But if I had it to do all over again, I would have hired a coach. I now know that many of the mistakes I made were avoidable. I could have achieved better, faster results if I had the benefit of proper guidance. I didn't have to go through the pain I endured. I could have emerged wealthier and healthier than I did.

There's a reason you are reading this book today. My journey taught me a great deal, and my purpose today is to share that knowledge with you. One of the things I love about FocalPoint is that each FocalPoint coach gets to select the area in which he practices. I coach small business owners because I know you. I *was* you. Now, I can offer you my personal experience and also all the power of the FocalPoint system. To you. For you.

Oh, how I wish I had met me twenty years ago.

Meet Your Coach

FocalPoint
Coaching & Training Excellence

Contact Me!

Patrick Clancey

pclancey@focalpointcoaching.com

patrickclancey.focalpointcoaching.com

As a young man, I was blessed to be awarded a full-tuition scholarship to the university of my choice. My scholarship featured the added bonus of providing a mentor who had previously studied the same major at that same school. This experience exposed me to the value of mentoring and started me on my avocation of mentoring and coaching those whose life journey is following the same course as mine. The education I received launched me into a business career that led me across industries and around the world, gaining valuable business insights and experience. My later-life role as a volunteer in the field of addiction recovery underscored my passion for serving others by building community and sharing my personal gifts. As a Certified FocalPoint Business Coach, I'm fortunate to be living in the space where my avocation, my experience, and my passion meet. I can help you find the sweet spot in your life, too!

Chapter 8

Let's Get Started!
(How Do We Begin?)

"If what you are doing is not moving you toward your goals, then it's moving you away from your goals."—Brian Tracy

Let's face it, if you weren't already something close to brilliant, you wouldn't still be running your own business. Success isn't easy, and there are a million ways to fail. I'm not saying that there aren't plenty of very smart people working in large corporations, but if you run a small company and that company is still in business, you have a lot on the ball!

You heard all those people who for years have been saying, "You bake amazing pies," or, "You write such elegant software," or, "Your infectious passion for imagining green solutions should be turned into a business." And you listened. You did something about it. You swallowed hard, gathered the courage, and took the leap. Your journey has validated that your talents *are* special and working for yourself *is* exhilarating. But it isn't all gazing at rainbows as you stroll through the park, either. There are plenty of challenges that you likely didn't imagine before you began. Some of those are in your wheelhouse, others less so.

No one is saying that you can't tackle all of it. I'm pretty sure you can because the person who has enough push to start a business has enough push to find solutions. It really isn't about whether you can find a way forward, it's about how hard the process is going to be and how far you are ultimately going to be able to go, given that struggling forward saps your energy.

If you have a hammer, nails, and enough lumber, I have no doubt you can build your house. But wouldn't the whole process be easier if you had a few power tools? Your coach has the power tools to get you where you want to go faster and easier than you might reach on your own. And who knows: If you aren't so exhausted, you might have the energy to build an even larger house! You already have the dream and you are already committed to the cause. All you need to do now is decide: Do you want to work harder or smarter?

An old Chinese proverb says, "The best time to plant a tree was twenty years ago. The second-best time is today." It is possible to have a great business and a great personal life. Having both was always the goal, right? So, let's make it happen. Your cellphone is in your pocket. It's time to yell, "Yo, Coach!"

"Think of a pebble dropping on a pond. Our coaches are the pebble, the splash made is the impact we have with our clients, and the ripples are the continuous impact we have in the business, people, and communities we serve."—Steve Thompson, Global President and CEO of FocalPoint

Acknowledgments

My praise and thanks go to Jennifer Bright, the "Book Doula," for her unwavering certainty that this book was "already written" somewhere deep inside of me. She convinced me that this project needed doing and that I was the one to do it. Then, in a manner reminiscent of any good coach, she held my feet to the fire until that goal was reached. Jennifer, your calm demeanor and nurturing style brought to life something I never thought existed.

Next, I'd like to say thank you to the team at the FocalPoint Head Office for helping me navigate the legal and intellectual property challenges that are inherent in writing a book about a process that is so deeply intertwined with a particular corporate entity.

A big shout out goes to Steve Thomson for convincing me that I was born to be a coach even before I ever became one. And for looking me straight in the eye and telling me that Patrick Clancey WILL change people's lives. Thank you, Steve for making me believe!

"Coach Patrick" certainly owes a huge debt of gratitude to the FocalPoint Training Team including but not limited to Margaret Maclay, Trisha Stetzel, Grant Fisher, Jim Masters, Rich Scott, Stephen Doyle, Eric Eurich, and Jim Diebold who imbued me with the "Competence & Confidence" that every coach needs to succeed. I'd also like to thank the FocalPoint Front Office Team & Marketing Department for supporting both my practice and me personally, my Practice Mentor Mark Steinke for his ongoing sagacious guidance, Ian Hayman for the wisdom of his Fireside Chats, and all of my fellow FocalPoint colleagues and coaches whose collective assistance is beyond recounting.

Deep thanks are owed to John Leonard, James W. Shannon, A. Paul Flask, and James E. Connell for the kindness, wisdom, faith, and guidance they showed to a young man who had the earmarks to become a solid business leader and for guiding me to get there. Your individual legacies live on!

No thanks would be complete without acknowledging my beloved parents and siblings who have walked with me every step of my life and who have supported me through every mistake as well as every success. I am extremely proud to be a small part of such an amazing family!

And, finally, I'd like to thank each of my clients who continually support me, challenge me and inspire me to be the best "non-equity partner" I can possibly be. Because of you, I have the most amazing job in the world!

About FocalPoint Coaching

FocalPoint Business Coaching is powered by founder Brian Tracy. Brian Tracy and business partner Campbell Fraser have adapted the very best of Brian's entrepreneurial and professional development learnings and strategy into the FocalPoint coaching and training process. This allows business owners, leaders and their teams to effectively leverage Brian's business building tools, systems, and methodology for maximum benefit through FocalPoint's more than 200 business coaches and trainers.

FocalPoint's vision is to lead leaders to optimize their overall business performance and reach their fullest potential. We guide our clients to bring forth possibilities never before imagined. We prioritize eliminating uncertainty, stress, and frustration so our clients can achieve a better balance in their lives. We are the "Pebble on the Pond." We impact the world first through our clients, then their employees, their families, their communities, and ultimately the world.

About the Author

Patrick Clancey brings more than 30 years of entrepreneurial business experience to his coaching practice. A trained chemical engineer, he has owned companies in the highway safety, broadband switchgear, software, and consulting fields. He has first-hand experience in the international arena, having worked or lived in Europe, Latin America, and Asia. Patrick also holds an MBA from the Haas School of Business at the University of California, Berkeley, where he focused on international marketing.

Patrick is active in the addiction recovery space and volunteers as an accredited facilitator, both in the United States and internationally. A person of faith, he is an active member and volunteer in his local church community. After nearly a lifetime abroad, Patrick has settled in the Lehigh Valley with his wife and a home full of animals. He coaches clients in many industries, from start-ups to approximately $20 million in annual revenue, regardless of geographic location.

Printed in the USA
CPSIA information can be obtained
at www.ICGtesting.com
CBHW080135270324
5919CB00008B/21

9 781958 711910